making
bread at home

Simple and delicious recipes for breads, cakes,
pizzas and pastries, at the touch of a button.

LINDA DOESER

This is a Parragon Publishing Book
This edition published in 2004

Parragon Publishing
Queen Street House
4 Queen Street
Bath BA1 1HE, UK

Produced by The Bridgewater Book Company Ltd

Photographer **Calvey Taylor-Haw**
Home economist **Michaela Jester**

Hardback ISBN: 1-40543-796-0

Printed in China

Notes

• This book uses both metric and imperial measurements. Follow
the same units of measurement throughout; do not mix metric
and imperial.

• All spoon measurements are level: teaspoons are assumed to be 5 ml
and tablespoons are assumed to be 15 ml.

CONTENTS

INTRODUCTION

There can be few more appetizing aromas than the smell of bread baking and few more delicious tastes than a still-warm, freshly baked loaf. With a bread machine, this can quickly become a trouble-free, everyday treat. If you have a timer delay, fresh bread every morning is even less bother than brewing a pot of coffee.

The recipes in this book cover all kinds of bread for every occasion and lifestyle. There are simple, basic breads that require no more effort than measuring a few ingredients into the machine and pressing the start switch, yet even these provide a wide range of flavors, from a plain white loaf to a moist fruit bread. More ambitious cooks can use the bread machine to take the hard work out of making the dough, and create

professional-looking plaits, baguettes, rolls, breadsticks, and Danish. The bread machine's versatility is further explored with mouth-watering pizza recipes, as well as some fabulous cakes to perk up mid-morning coffee or an afternoon snack.

ABOUT BREAD MACHINES

Although a bread machine is easy to use it must be treated with care. Here are some tips for working a bread machine for the best results.

Make sure that the kneading blade is firmly attached. Do not plug the machine in until you are ready to switch it on. Always remove the bread pan to add the ingredients to avoid spills inside the machine.

Add the ingredients in the order listed unless instructed otherwise. Measure ingredients accurately.

Add ingredients such as eggs at room temperature. Use hand-hot liquid—but no hotter—as this will activate the yeast. Make sure that flours and yeast are not past their 'use-by' dates.

Do not open the bread machine during cooking, except when necessary for adding extra ingredients, such as dried fruit. Otherwise, the temperature will drop and the bread will be disappointing.

Use oven gloves to remove the bread pan after baking—it will be very hot. Make sure the bread machine is on a level surface and cannot be reached by young children.

Do not use the timer delay for recipes that include perishable ingredients, such as eggs, yogurt, or buttermilk.

The recipes have been tested in medium-sized machines. They are all suitable for large machines and most will work successfully in small machines. Check the manufacturer's handbook for maximum capacity.

For shaped loaves, follow the instructions for proving the dough (letting it rise). Put in a warm place, such as an airing cupboard. The dough may take longer to rise in a cooler place. If you need to use a conventional oven, preheat the oven fully before baking.

The kneading blade should be well-seated in the bottom of the bread pan.

Make sure that you add the ingredients in the order given by the recipe.

Check that the bread pan is sitting securely in the machine before kneading begins.

BASIC BREADS

Here are easy recipes for a wide range of basic breads. For the simplest you just add the ingredients to the bread machine, press start, and turn out a perfect loaf to cool. Varying the ingredients produces a delicious selection of breads, from a healthy Harvest Loaf to a tasty Corn Bread. There are also popular breads and rolls such as White Rolls and Pittas for cooking in a conventional oven. Use the bread machine to make perfect dough, then turn out and shape before baking. You will find that more specialist breads, such as Plaited Poppy Seed Bread and Baguettes, are well within the scope of the beginner.

CRUSTY LOAF

INGREDIENTS
1 egg
1 egg yolk
hand-hot water, as required
3¾ cups white bread flour
1½ tsp salt
2 tsp sugar
2 tbsp butter, softened
   or diced
1 tsp easy-blend dried yeast

1 Remove the bread pan from the bread machine. Put the egg and egg yolk into a measuring jug and beat lightly to mix; then add sufficient hand-hot water to make up to 10 fl oz/300 ml. Stir to mix. Pour into the bread pan.

2 Sprinkle the flour over the liquid so that it is completely covered. Place the salt, sugar, and butter in 3 corners of the pan. Make an indentation in the flour with your finger without exposing the liquid and add the yeast to it.

3 Fit the bread pan in the machine and close the lid. Set the bread machine to the basic setting, medium crust, and press start.

4 When the cycle has finished, switch off the machine. Remove the bread pan with oven gloves and turn out the bread on to a wire rack to cool. Remove the kneading blade, if necessary.

MILK BREAD

INGREDIENTS

⁷⁄₈ cup hand-hot full cream
    or semi-skimmed milk
generous ¹⁄₃ cup hand-hot water
3½ cups white bread flour

1½ tsp salt
2 tsp sugar
2 tbsp butter, softened or diced
1 tsp easy-blend dried yeast

1 Remove the bread pan from the bread machine. Pour the milk and water into the bread pan.

2 Sprinkle the flour over the liquid so that it is completely covered. Place the salt, sugar, and butter in 3 corners of the pan. Make an indentation in the flour with your finger without exposing the liquid and add the yeast to it.

3 Fit the bread pan in the machine and close the lid. Set the bread machine to the basic setting, medium crust, and press start.

4 When the cycle has finished, switch off the machine. Remove the bread pan with oven gloves and turn out the bread on to a wire rack to cool. Remove the kneading blade, if necessary.

HARVEST LOAF

INGREDIENTS
¾ cup hand-hot water
1½ tbsp sunflower oil
1½ cups whole wheat
   bread flour
1 tbsp nonfat milk powder
1 tsp salt
2 tbsp soft brown sugar
1 tsp easy-blend dried yeast

1 Remove the bread pan from the bread machine. Pour the water into the bread pan and add the sunflower oil.

2 Sprinkle the flour over the liquid so that it is completely covered, then sprinkle in the nonfat dry milk powder. Place the salt and sugar in 2 corners of the pan. Make an indentation in the flour with your finger without exposing the liquid and add the yeast to it.

3 Fit the bread pan in the machine and close the lid. Set the bread machine to the whole wheat setting, medium crust, and press start.

4 When the cycle has finished, switch off the machine. Remove the bread pan with oven gloves and turn out the bread on to a wire rack to cool. Remove the kneading blade, if necessary.

CORN BREAD

INGREDIENTS
²/₃ cup hand-hot water
5 tbsp hand-hot milk
1 tbsp corn oil
scant 2 cups white bread flour
³/₄ cup fine cornmeal
1 tsp salt
1½ tsp light brown sugar
1 tsp easy-blend dried yeast

Topping
1 tbsp water
1 tbsp medium cornmeal

1 Remove the bread pan from the bread machine. Pour in the water, milk, and corn oil.

2 Sprinkle the flour over the liquid so that it is completely covered, then sprinkle in the cornmeal. Place the salt and sugar in 2 corners of the pan. Make an indentation in the flour with your finger without exposing the liquid and add the yeast to it.

3 Fit the bread pan in the machine and close the lid. Set the bread machine to the quick setting, medium crust, and press start. About 5 minutes before baking begins (about 20 minutes from the start), add the topping. Brush the top of the dough with the water and carefully sprinkle with the medium cornmeal.

4 When the cycle has finished, switch off the machine. Remove the bread pan with oven gloves and turn out the bread on to a wire rack to cool. Remove the kneading blade if necessary.

WHITE ROLLS

INGREDIENTS
⅝ cup hand-hot water
⅝ cup hand-hot milk
3½ cups white bread flour, plus
    extra for dusting
1½ tsp salt
2 tsp superfine sugar
1 tsp easy-blend dried yeast
sunflower oil, for greasing
milk, for glazing

1 Remove the bread pan from the bread machine. Pour the water and milk into the bread pan. Sprinkle the flour over the liquid so that it is completely covered. Place the salt and sugar in 2 corners of the pan. Make an indentation in the flour with your finger without exposing the liquid and add the yeast to it.

2 Fit the bread pan in the machine and close the lid. Set the bread machine to the dough setting and press start.

3 When the cycle has finished, switch off the machine and remove the bread pan. Lightly flour a work surface and remove the dough from the pan. Knock back gently, then divide it into 10 equal pieces. Place on a tray and cover with lightly oiled plastic wrap.

4 Lightly oil 2 cookie sheets. Take a piece of dough from underneath the plastic wrap, shape it into a ball, then place on a lightly floured surface and roll out into a 4–inch/10–cm–long oval. Roll out the other pieces in the same way, place on the cookie sheets and cover with lightly oiled plastic wrap. Set aside in a warm place for 30 minutes to rise.

5 Remove the plastic wrap and gently press the center of each roll with 2 fingers to release any large air bubbles, then brush the tops with milk and dust with a little flour. Bake in a preheated oven, 400°F/200°C, for 15–20 minutes, until lightly browned. Transfer the rolls to wire racks to cool slightly. Serve warm.

BAGUETTES

INGREDIENTS
1⅜ cups hand-hot water
3½ cups white bread flour,
   plus extra for dusting
1½ tsp salt
1½ tsp easy-blend dried yeast
sunflower oil, for greasing

1 Remove the bread pan from the bread machine. Pour the water into the bread pan. Sprinkle the flour over the liquid so that it is completely covered. Place the salt in 1 corner of the pan. Make an indentation in the flour with your finger without exposing the liquid and add the yeast to it.

2 Fit the bread pan in the machine and close the lid. Set the bread machine to the French dough setting and press start. If your machine has only a French bread baking setting, remove the dough after the final rising (about 2 hours and 55 minutes from the start).

3 When the cycle has finished, switch off the machine and remove the bread pan. Lightly flour a work surface and remove the dough from the pan. Knock back, then divide into 2 equal pieces. Shape each piece into a ball, then roll out each ball to a 8 x 3–inch/20 x 7.5–cm rectangle. With the long side of a rectangle facing you, fold the top third of dough down and the bottom third up and press together. Set aside to rest while you fold the second rectangle. Then repeat twice more with each rectangle, leaving them to rest in between each folding.

4 Lightly flour and pleat 2 dish towels. Gently roll and stretch each piece of dough, in turn, into a stick about 12 inches/30 cm long. Place each baguette between the pleats of a dish towel to support it and cover with lightly oiled plastic wrap. Set aside in a warm place for 30–40 minutes to rise.

5 Lightly oil a cookie sheet. Remove the plastic wrap and gently roll the loaves from the dish towels on to the cookie sheet, spaced well apart. Make several diagonal slashes on the tops, with a sharp knife. Set the oven at 450°F/230°C. Spray the inside of the preheated oven with water and bake the loaves for 15–20 minutes, until crusty and golden. Transfer to a wire rack to cool.

BREADSTICKS WITH SESAME SEEDS

INGREDIENTS
7/8 cup hand-hot water
3 tbsp olive oil, plus extra for
  greasing and brushing
2½ cups white bread flour, plus
  extra for dusting
1½ tsp salt
1½ tsp easy-blend dried yeast
sesame seeds, for coating

1 Remove the bread pan from the bread machine. Pour the water into the bread pan and add the olive oil. Sprinkle the flour over the liquid so that it is completely covered. Place the salt in 1 corner of the bread pan. Make an indentation in the flour with your finger without exposing the liquid and add the yeast to it.

2 Fit the bread pan in the machine and close the lid. Set the bread machine to the dough setting and press start.

3 When the cycle has finished, switch off the machine and remove the bread pan. Lightly flour a work surface and remove the dough from the pan. Knock back and roll out to a 9 x 8–inch/23 x 20–cm rectangle. Cut the dough into 3 strips, each 8 inches/20 cm long, then cut each strip across into 10 equal pieces.

4 Gently roll and stretch each piece of dough into a stick about 12 inches/30 cm long. Lightly oil 2 cookie sheets. Spread out the sesame seeds on a large, shallow plate or tray. Roll each breadstick in the sesame seeds to coat, then place on the cookie sheets, spaced well apart. Brush with olive oil, cover with plastic wrap and set aside in a warm place for 15 minutes.

5 Remove the plastic wrap and bake the breadsticks in a preheated oven, 400°F/200°C, for 10 minutes. Turn them over, return to the oven and bake for a further 5–10 minutes, until golden. Transfer to a wire rack to cool.

PITTAS

INGREDIENTS
generous ⅞ cup hand-hot water
2½ cups white bread flour, plus
    extra for dusting
1½ tsp salt
1 tsp sugar
1 tsp easy-blend dried yeast
1 tbsp olive oil, plus extra for greasing

1 Remove the bread pan from the bread machine and pour in the water and the olive oil. Sprinkle the flour over the liquid so that it is completely covered. Place the salt and sugar in 2 corners of the pan. Make an indentation in the flour with your finger without exposing the liquid and add the yeast to it.

2 Fit the bread pan in the machine and close the lid. Set the bread machine to the pizza dough setting and press start. (If your machine does not have a pizza dough setting, refer to the manufacturer's handbook to check whether you should use the dough setting or the cake setting. If using the cake setting, switch off the machine at the end of the final rising—about 1 hour and 40 minutes from the start.)

3 When the cycle has finished, switch off the machine and remove the bread pan. Lightly oil a cookie sheet. Lightly flour a work surface and remove the dough from the pan. Knock back gently, then divide into 6 equal pieces. Shape each piece into a ball and place on the cookie sheet. Cover with oiled plastic wrap and set aside for 10 minutes. Meanwhile, place 2 or 3 cookie sheets in the oven and preheat to 450°F/230°C.

4 Uncover the dough and flatten each piece slightly. Roll out each piece on a lightly floured surface into a round. Sprinkle lightly with flour and cover with plastic wrap. Set aside for a further 10 minutes to rest. Remove the plastic wrap. Transfer the dough rounds to the hot cookie sheets, spaced well apart, and bake for 5 minutes, until risen and golden. Transfer to a wire rack to cool.

PLAITED POPPY SEED BREAD

INGREDIENTS

¾ cup hand-hot water

2 tbsp sunflower oil, plus
   extra for greasing

1½ cups white bread flour,
   plus extra for dusting

2 tbsp nonfat dry milk powder

1 tsp salt

1¼ tbsp sugar

1 tsp easy-blend dried yeast

3 tbsp poppy seeds

Topping

1 egg yolk

1 tbsp milk

1 tbsp superfine sugar

2 tbsp poppy seeds

1 Remove the bread pan from the bread machine. Pour in the water and add the sunflower oil. Sprinkle the flour over the liquid so that it is completely covered, then sprinkle in the nonfat dry milk powder. Place the salt and sugar in 2 corners of the pan. Make an indentation in the flour with your finger without exposing the liquid and add the yeast to it.

2 Fit the bread pan in the machine and close the lid. Set the bread machine to the dough setting and press start. When the machine beeps for extra ingredients, or 5 minutes before the end of kneading, add the poppy seeds.

3 When the cycle has finished, switch off the machine and remove the bread pan. Lightly flour a work surface and remove the dough from the pan. Knock back gently and knead lightly for 1–2 minutes.

4 Oil a cookie sheet. Divide the dough into 3 equal pieces and shape each piece into a rope about 10–12 inches/25–30 cm long. Place the ropes side by side and pinch them together at one end. Plait the

dough, and pinch the other end together, tucking it underneath. Place the plait on the cookie sheet, cover with lightly oiled plastic wrap and set aside in a warm place for about 30 minutes to rise.

5 To make the topping, lightly beat the egg yolk with the milk and superfine sugar to combine. Remove the plastic wrap from the plait, brush the top with the egg glaze and sprinkle over the poppy seeds. Bake in a preheated oven, 400°F/200°C, for 30–35 minutes, until the loaf is golden and sounds hollow when tapped. Transfer to a wire rack to cool.

BREAKFAST BRIOCHE

INGREDIENTS

2 eggs, at room temperature
2 tbsp hand-hot milk
1½ cups white bread flour, plus
    extra for dusting
½ tsp salt
1 tbsp superfine sugar
4 tbsp butter, melted
1½ tsp easy-blend dried yeast
sunflower oil, for greasing

Glaze
1 egg yolk
1 tbsp milk or water

1 Remove the bread pan from the bread machine. Lightly beat the eggs with the milk in a bowl, then pour into the bread pan. Sprinkle the flour over the liquid so that it is completely covered. Place the salt, sugar, and melted butter in 3 corners of the pan. Make an indentation in the flour with your finger without exposing the liquid and add the yeast to it.

2 Fit the bread pan in the machine and close the lid. Set the bread machine to the dough setting and press start. When the cycle has finished, switch off the machine. Leave the dough in the machine, with the lid shut, for an extra 30 minutes, or until the dough is well risen.

3 Remove the bread pan. Lightly flour a work surface and remove the dough from the pan. Knock back gently. Slice off one-quarter of the dough, wrap in oiled plastic wrap and set aside. Oil a brioche mold. Knead the large piece of dough lightly and shape into a ball. Place in the mold and make an indentation or cut a cross in the top with a sharp knife. Unwrap and lightly knead the reserved dough, shape into a round, then elongate slightly to a rough pear shape. Place the pear-shaped dough on top of the larger ball of dough, narrow end downward. Cover with lightly oiled plastic wrap and set aside in a warm place for about 1 hour to rise.

4 Remove the plastic wrap. To make the glaze, lightly beat the egg yolk with the milk, then brush over the top of the brioche. Bake in a preheated oven, 425°F/ 220°C, for 40–45 minutes, until risen and golden. Transfer to a wire rack to cool. Serve warm or cold.

HEALTHY SNACKS

These substantial flavor-packed loaves provide a delicious and healthy snack. They also add the perfect touch to a picnic, lunch, or party. Potatoes, cheese, and yogurt can all be easily incorporated into the dough to create loaves such as Oatmeal and Potato Bread, Cheesy Chive Granary Bread, or Whole Wheat Yogurt Bread, which will liven up any meal. Naan with coriander is an excellent addition to a main course if you are preparing a curry, but it can also be baked as a lunchtime snack as an alternative to rolls or loaves.

OATMEAL AND POTATO BREAD

INGREDIENTS

8 oz/225 g floury potatoes
   (peeled weight)
generous ⅞ cup hand-hot
   water
3¾ cups white bread flour
3 tbsp rolled oats
2 tbsp nonfat dry milk powder
1½ tsp salt

1½ tbsp dark brown sugar
3 tbs butter, softened
   or diced
1½ tsp easy-blend dried yeast

Topping
1 tbsp water
1 tbsp rolled oats

1 Place the potatoes in a large pan, add water to cover, bring to the boil and cook for 20–25 minutes, until tender. Drain, then mash until smooth. Cool.

2 Remove the bread pan from the bread machine. Pour in the water. Sprinkle the flour over the liquid so that it is completely covered, then sprinkle in the oats and nonfat dry milk powder. Add the mashed potatoes to the bread pan, then place the salt, sugar, and butter in 3 corners of the pan. Make an indention in the flour with your finger without exposing the liquid and add the yeast to it.

3 Fit the bread pan in the machine and close the lid. Set the bread machine to the basic setting, medium crust, and press start. About 5 minutes before the end of the final rising cycle (about 1¼ hours from the start), add the topping. Brush the surface of the loaf with the water and carefully sprinkle over the rolled oats.

4 When the cycle has finished, switch off the machine. Remove the bread pan with oven gloves and turn out the bread on to a wire rack to cool. Remove the kneading blade if necessary.

RYE AND SEED BREAD

INGREDIENTS

generous 1½ cups hand-hot water

2 tbsp sunflower oil

2½ tbsp molasses

1¾ cups white bread flour

1 cup rye flour

¾ cup whole wheat flour

generous ½ cup dried breadcrumbs

3 tbsp oat bran

1½ tsp salt

1½ tbsp cocoa powder

2 tsp caraway seeds

½ tsp easy-blend dried yeast

1 Remove the bread pan from the bread machine. Pour the water into the bread pan and add the oil and molasses.

2 Sprinkle all 3 types of flour over the liquid so that it is completely covered, then sprinkle in the breadcrumbs and oat bran. Place the salt, cocoa powder, and caraway seeds in 3 corners of the pan. Make an indentation in the flour with your finger without exposing the liquid and add the yeast to it.

3 Fit the bread pan in the machine and close the lid. Set the bread machine to the whole wheat setting, medium crust, and press start.

4 When the cycle has finished, switch off the machine. Remove the bread pan with oven gloves and turn out the bread on to a wire rack to cool. Remove the kneading blade if necessary.

WHOLE WHEAT YOGURT BREAD

INGREDIENTS

2/3 cup hand-hot water
1/2 cup natural yogurt, at
  room temperature
1 tbsp sunflower oil
1 tbsp molasses or corn syrup
1 1/4 cups white bread flour
1 1/8 cups whole wheat
  bread flour
1/2 cup wheat bran
1 tsp salt
3/4 tsp easy-blend dried yeast

1 Remove the bread pan from the bread machine. Pour in the water and add the yogurt, sunflower oil, and molasses.

2 Sprinkle both types of flour over the liquid so that it is completely covered. Place the wheat bran and salt in 2 corners of the pan. Make an indentation in the flour with your finger without exposing the liquid and add the yeast to it.

3 Fit the bread pan in the machine and close the lid. Set the bread machine to the basic setting, medium crust, and press start.

4 When the cycle has finished, switch off the machine. Remove the bread pan with oven gloves and turn out the bread on to a wire rack to cool. Remove the kneading blade if necessary.

PARSLEY AND CHIVE COTTAGE LOAF

INGREDIENTS

1¼ cups hand-hot water
3½ cups white bread flour, plus
   extra for dusting
1½ tsp salt
1½ tsp sugar
1½ tsp easy-blend dried yeast
2 tbsp chopped fresh parsley

2 tbsp chopped fresh chives
1 tbsp chopped fresh thyme
sunflower oil, for greasing

Glaze
1 tbsp water
1 tbsp salt

1 Remove the bread pan from the bread machine. Pour the water into the bread pan. Sprinkle the flour over the liquid so that it is completely covered. Place the salt and sugar in 2 corners of the pan. Make an indentation in the flour with your finger without exposing the liquid and add the yeast to it.

2 Fit the bread pan in the machine and close the lid. Set the bread machine to the dough setting. When the machine beeps, or 5 minutes before the end of kneading, add all the herbs.

3 When the cycle has finished, switch off the machine and remove the bread pan. Lightly flour 2 cookie sheets and a work surface. Remove the dough from the pan. Knock back gently, then cut off one-third of the dough. Shape each piece of dough into a ball and place on the cookie sheets. Cover with oiled plastic wrap and set aside in a warm place for 30 minutes to rise.

4 Unwrap the dough and cut a cross in the top of the larger piece with a sharp knife. Brush with water and place the smaller piece on top. Oil the handle of a wooden spoon and push it through both balls of dough. Cover the loaf with oiled plastic wrap and set aside in a warm place for 10 minutes to rise.

5 To make the glaze, pour the water into a small bowl and stir in the salt. Remove the plastic wrap and brush the loaf with the glaze. Make a series of slashes around the top and bottom of the loaf with a sharp knife, and dust with flour. Bake in a preheated oven, 425°F/220°C, for 30–35 minutes, until the loaf is golden and sounds hollow when tapped on the base. Transfer to a wire rack to cool.

CHEESY CHIVE GRANARY BREAD

INGREDIENTS

scant ⁷/₈ cup hand-hot water
1 egg, beaten lightly
5 tbsp ricotta cheese, beaten until smooth
³/₈ cup Granary flour
3 cups white bread flour, plus extra for dusting
1 tsp salt
2 tsp sugar

1¹/₂ tsp easy-blend dried yeast
3 oz/85 g dolcelatte cheese, diced finely
3 oz/85 g freshly grated Emmental cheese
3 tbsp finely chopped fresh chives
sunflower oil, for greasing
2 tbsp freshly grated Parmesan cheese

1 Remove the bread pan from the bread machine. Pour the water into the bread pan and add the egg and ricotta. Sprinkle both types of flour over the liquid so that it is completely covered. Place the salt and sugar in 2 corners of the pan. Make an indentation in the flour without exposing the liquid and add the yeast to it.

2 Fit the bread pan in the machine and close the lid. Set the bread machine to the dough setting. When the machine beeps for extra ingredients, or 5 minutes before the end of kneading, add the dolcelatte, Emmental and chives.

3 When the cycle has finished, switch off the machine and remove the bread pan. Lightly flour a work surface and remove the dough from the pan. Knock back gently, then shape into a round, 8 inches/ 20 cm in diameter. Place on an oiled cookie sheet, cover with oiled plastic wrap and set aside in a warm place for 40–45 minutes to rise.

4 Remove the plastic wrap. Sprinkle over the Parmesan. Bake in a preheated oven, 400°F/200°C, for 40–45 minutes, until the loaf is golden and sounds hollow when tapped on the base. Transfer to a wire rack to cool.

NAAN WITH GARLIC AND CORIANDER

INGREDIENTS

generous ⅓ cup hand-hot water
4 tbsp natural yogurt
scant 2 cups white bread flour
1 garlic clove, chopped finely
1 tsp ground coriander
1 tsp salt

2 tsp clear honey
1 tbsp ghee or butter, melted, plus
   extra for brushing
1 tsp easy-blend dried yeast
sunflower oil, for greasing
1 tsp black onion seeds
1 tbsp chopped fresh coriander

1 Remove the bread pan from the bread machine. Pour the water into the bread pan and add the yogurt. Sprinkle the flour over the liquid so that it is completely covered, then sprinkle in the garlic and ground coriander. Place the salt, honey and melted ghee in 3 corners of the pan. Make an indentation in the flour with your finger without exposing the liquid and add the yeast to it.

2 Fit the bread pan in the machine and close the lid. Set the bread machine to the dough setting or pizza dough setting and press start.

3 When the cycle has finished, switch off the machine and remove the bread pan. Place 3 cookie sheets in the oven to preheat to 475°F/240°C. Lightly flour a work surface and remove the dough from the pan. Knock back gently and divide into 3 pieces. Shape each piece into a ball and cover 2 of them with oiled plastic wrap.

4 Roll out the uncovered piece of dough into a teardrop shape about ⅜ inch/8 mm thick. Cover with oiled plastic wrap, then roll out the other pieces of dough in turn.

5 Place the naan on the hot cookie sheets and sprinkle with the onion seeds and chopped coriander. Bake for about 5 minutes, until puffed up. Place under a preheated grill for a few seconds, until beginning to brown and blister. Brush with melted ghee and serve warm.

MIXED SEED BREAD

INGREDIENTS

1¼ cups hand-hot water
1½ tbsp sunflower oil
2 tsp lemon juice
generous 2½ cups white bread flour
⅞ cup rye flour
1½ tbsp nonfat dry milk powder

1½ tsp salt
1 tbsp light brown sugar
1 tsp caraway seeds
½ tsp poppy seeds
½ tsp sesame seeds
1 tsp easy-blend dried yeast

Topping
1 egg white
1 tbsp water
1 tbsp sunflower or
   pumpkin seeds

1 Remove the bread pan from the bread machine. Pour in the water and add the sunflower oil and lemon juice. Sprinkle both types of flour over the liquid so that it is completely covered, then sprinkle in the nonfat dry milk powder. Place the salt, sugar, and seeds in 3 corners of the pan. Make an indentation in the flour with your finger without exposing the liquid and add the yeast to it.

2 Fit the bread pan in the machine and close the lid. Set the bread machine to the basic setting, medium crust, and press start.

3 To make the topping, lightly beat the egg white with the water to make a glaze. Just before the baking cycle starts (about 2 hours after the start), brush the glaze over the loaf, then gently press the sunflower or pumpkin seeds all over the top.

4 When the cycle has finished, switch off the machine. Remove the bread pan with oven gloves and turn out the bread on to a wire rack to cool. Remove the kneading blade if necessary.

FRUIT AND NUT BREADS

Fruits and nuts give breads some wonderful textures and flavors. In this chapter, dried or fresh fruits and a variety of nuts are used to produce an appetizing selection of breads, cakes, and pastries that are a perfect treat at any time of the day. Why not try Marmalade Bread or Orange and Banana Bread for that fruity tang, or if you prefer a mixture of fruit and nuts, choose the Walnut and Apple Streusel? For a lovely malty bread try the Malted Fruit Loaf, while the Walnut Loaf is a sophisticated nut bread enhanced by the flavor of different herbs.

APRICOT MUESLI BREAD

INGREDIENTS

1 cup hand-hot water

2 tbsp sunflower oil, plus extra
   for greasing

1 tbsp clear honey

2 cups white bread flour

1/2 cup whole wheat bread flour, plus
   extra for dusting

1 1/4 cup unsweetened muesli

3 tbsp nonfat dry milk powder

1 1/2 tsp salt

1 1/2 tsp easy-blend dried yeast

2 1/2 oz/70 g ready-to-eat dried
   apricots, chopped

1 Remove the bread pan from the bread machine. Put the water, sunflower oil, and honey into the bread pan. Sprinkle both types of flour over the liquid to cover it completely, then sprinkle in the muesli and nonfat dry milk powder. Place the salt in 1 corner of the pan. Make an indentation in the flour with your finger without exposing the liquid and add the yeast to it.

2 Fit the bread pan in the machine and close the lid. Set the bread machine to the dough setting and press start. When the machine beeps for extra ingredients, or 5 minutes before the end of kneading, add the dried apricots.

3 When the cycle has finished, switch off the machine and remove the bread pan. Lightly oil a cookie sheet. Lightly flour a work surface with whole wheat flour and remove the dough from the pan. Knock back gently, then shape into a round loaf. Place on the cookie sheet. Cut a deep cross in the top with a sharp knife. Cover with lightly oiled plastic wrap and set aside in a warm place for about 30–40 minutes to rise.

4 Remove the plastic wrap and bake the bread in a preheated oven, 400°F/200°C, for 30–35 minutes, until golden. Transfer to a wire rack to cool.

FIG AND ROSEMARY BREAD

INGREDIENTS

generous ⅔ cup hand-hot water
2 eggs, beaten lightly
4 tbsp olive oil
3¾ cups white bread flour
2 tbsp nonfat dry milk powder

1 tbsp finely chopped fresh rosemary
1½ tsp salt
2 tsp sugar
1 tsp easy-blend dried yeast
4 oz/115 g dried figs, chopped
  roughly

1 Remove the bread pan from the bread machine. Pour the water into the bread pan and add the eggs and olive oil.

2 Sprinkle the flour over the liquid so that it is completely covered, then sprinkle in the nonfat dry milk powder and the rosemary. Place the salt and sugar in 2 corners of the pan. Make an indentation in the flour with your finger without exposing the liquid and add the yeast to it.

3 Fit the bread pan in the machine and close the lid. Set the bread machine to the basic setting, medium crust, and press start. When the machine beeps for extra ingredients, or 5 minutes before the end of kneading, add the figs.

4 When the cycle has finished, switch off the machine. Remove the bread pan with oven gloves and turn out the bread on to a wire rack to cool. Remove the kneading blade if necessary.

ORANGE AND BANANA BREAD

INGREDIENTS

4 tbsp orange juice

$^7/_8$ cup buttermilk or water

2 medium ripe bananas or 1 large ripe
   banana, peeled and mashed

3 tbsp clear honey

3$^3/_4$ cups white bread flour,
   plus extra 1–2 tbsp for
   sticky dough

1$^1/_2$ tbsp nonfat dry milk powder,
   optional

1 tsp salt

3 tbs butter, softened or diced

1 tsp easy-blend dried yeast

milk, for glazing, optional

1 Remove the bread pan from the bread machine. Pour the orange juice and hand-hot buttermilk or water into the bread pan. Add the mashed bananas and honey.

2 Sprinkle the flour over the liquid and fruit so that it is completely covered. If using water, sprinkle the nonfat dry milk powder over the flour, but do not add it if you have used buttermilk. Place the salt and butter in 2 corners of the bread pan. Make an indentation in the flour with your finger without exposing the liquid and add the yeast to it.

3 Fit the bread pan in the machine and close the lid. Set the bread machine to the basic setting, medium crust, and press start. If the dough looks very sticky toward the end of the first kneading, add a further 1–2 tablespoons of white bread flour. (The stickiness depends on the ripeness of the bananas.)

4 Just before the baking cycle starts (about 2 hours after the start), brush the top of the loaf with milk to glaze, if you like. When the cycle has finished, switch off the machine. Remove the bread pan with oven gloves and turn out the bread on to a wire rack to cool.

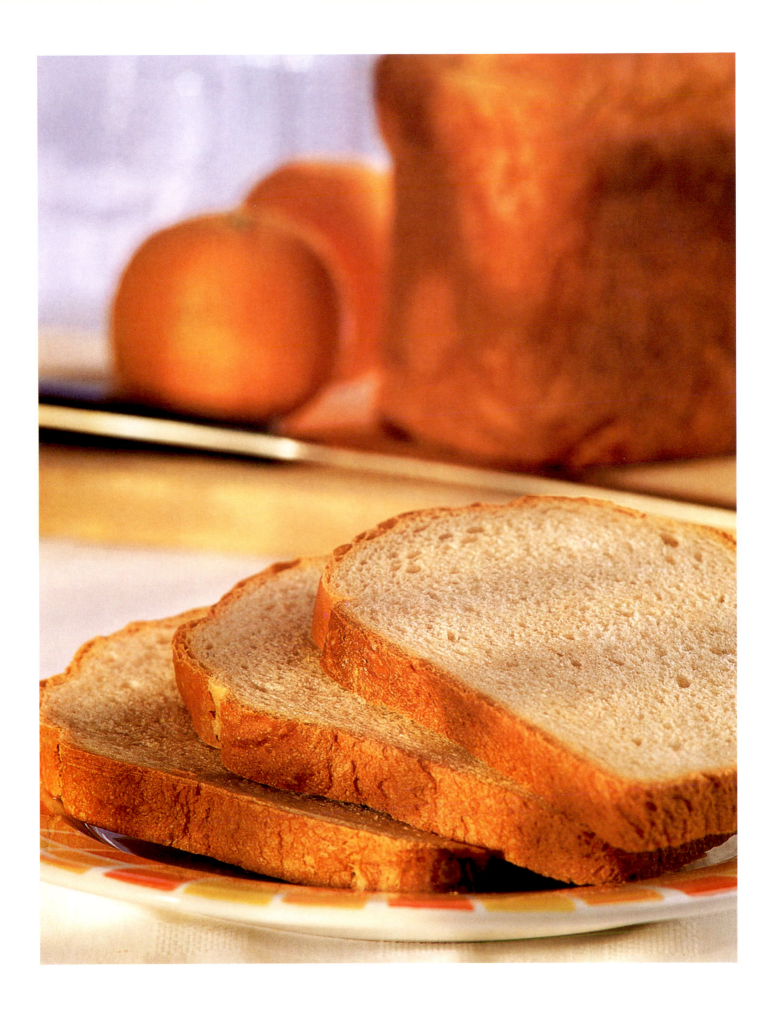

WALNUT AND APPLE STREUSEL

INGREDIENTS

generous ⅓ cup hand-hot milk
1 egg, beaten lightly
1¾ cups white bread flour, plus
   extra for dusting
½ tsp salt
3 tbsp superfine sugar
2 tbsp butter, melted
1 tsp easy-blend dried yeast
sunflower oil, for greasing

Topping
generous ¾ cup plain flour
4 tbsp butter, diced
2 oz/55 g walnuts, chopped finely
4 tbsp superfine sugar
1 tsp ground cinnamon
4 dessert apples
2 tbsp lemon juice

1 Remove the bread pan from the bread machine. Pour the milk into the bread pan and add the egg. Sprinkle the flour over the liquid so that it is completely covered. Place the salt, sugar, and butter in 3 corners of the pan. Make an indentation in the flour with your finger without exposing the liquid and add the yeast to it.

2 Fit the bread pan in the machine and close the lid. Set the bread machine to the dough setting and press start. Meanwhile, make the topping. Sift the flour into a bowl and add the butter. Rub in with your fingertips until the mixture resembles coarse bread crumbs. Stir in the walnuts, sugar, and cinnamon. Set aside until required.

3 When the cycle has finished, switch off the machine. Lightly grease a round 10-inch/ 25-cm-diameter springform cake pan Lightly flour a work surface and remove the dough from the bread pan. Knock back gently, then roll out into a round to fit the pan. Ease the dough into the pan.

4 Peel, core, and thinly slice the apples. Toss them in the lemon juice to prevent them from discoloring, then arrange in circles on top of the dough. Sprinkle the nut topping over them. Cover the cake with lightly oiled plastic wrap and set aside in a warm place for 25–30 minutes to rise. Remove the plastic wrap and bake the cake in a preheated oven, 375˚F/190˚C, for about 30 minutes, until golden. Leave in the pan to cool for 5 minutes, then transfer to a wire rack to cool completely.

CINNAMON AND APRICOT BUNS

INGREDIENTS

scant 1 cup hand-hot milk

1 egg, beaten lightly

3³/₄ cups white bread flour, plus
extra for dusting

¹/₂ tsp salt

scant ¹/₂ cup superfine sugar

4 tbsp butter, softened or diced

1 tsp easy-blend dried yeast

sunflower oil, for greasing

Filling

2 tsp butter, melted

4 oz/115 g ready-to-eat dried
apricots, chopped

2 oz/55 g golden raisins

2 tbsp light brown sugar

1¹/₂ tsp ground cinnamon

Glaze

4 tbsp water

4 tbsp superfine sugar

1 tsp Amaretto liqueur

1 Remove the bread pan from the bread machine. Pour the milk into the bread pan and add the egg. Sprinkle the flour over the liquid so that it is completely covered. Place the salt, sugar, and butter in 3 corners of the pan. Make an indentation in the flour with your finger without exposing the liquid and add the yeast to it.

2 Fit the bread pan in the machine and close the lid. Set the bread machine to the dough setting and press start. When the cycle has finished, switch off the machine and remove the bread pan. Lightly grease a 9–inch/23–cm square cake pan and lightly flour a work surface. Remove the dough from the pan and knock back gently. Roll out into a 12–inch/30–cm square. For the filling brush the surface of the dough with the melted butter, then sprinkle the apricots, golden raisins, sugar and cinnamon evenly over it, leaving a ¹/₂-inch/1-cm border on one edge.

3 Roll up the dough, like a Swiss roll, from the filling-covered edge to the uncovered edge. Press firmly to seal, then cut into 12 slices. Arrange the slices in the cake pan with the cut sides upward. Cover with lightly oiled plastic wrap and set aside in a warm place for about 45 minutes to rise. Remove the plastic wrap and bake the buns in a preheated oven, 400°F/200°C, for about 20 minutes, until golden brown. Leave in the pan to cool for 5 minutes, then turn out on to a wire rack.

4 Meanwhile, make the glaze. Heat the water and sugar in a small saucepan, stirring until the sugar has dissolved. Bring to a boil, then continue to boil, without stirring, for 1¹/₂–2 minutes, until syrupy. Stir in the liqueur and brush the syrup all over the buns. Serve warm or cold.

MARMALADE BREAD

INGREDIENTS

²/₃ cup hand-hot water

²/₃ cup hand-hot milk

2 tbsp sunflower oil, plus extra
   for greasing

3¹/₂ cups white bread flour, plus
   extra for dusting

1¹/₂ tsp salt

1¹/₂ tsp sugar

1¹/₂ tsp easy-blend dried yeast

7 tbsp orange marmalade

Topping

1 egg yolk

1 tbsp milk

1 tbsp superfine sugar

1–2 tbsp crystallized orange peel

1 Remove the bread pan from the bread machine. Pour the water and milk into the bread pan and add the oil. Sprinkle the flour over the liquid so that it is completely covered. Place the salt and sugar in 2 corners of the bread pan. Make an indentation in the flour with your finger without exposing the liquid and add the yeast to it.

2 Fit the bread pan in the machine and close the lid. Set the bread machine to the dough setting and press start.

3 When the cycle has finished, switch off the machine and remove the bread pan. Lightly flour a work surface and remove the dough from the pan. Knock back gently, then roll out into a 10 x 8-inch/ 25 x 20-cm rectangle about ³/₄ inch/ 2 cm thick.

4 Lightly grease a 10 x 4-inch/ 25 x 10-cm loaf pan with oil. Spread the marmalade evenly over the dough, leaving a ¹/₂-inch/1-cm border on one long edge.

5 Roll up the dough like a Swiss roll, from the filling-covered edge to the uncovered edge. Press firmly to seal, and place seam-side down in the pan. Cover with lightly oiled plastic wrap. Set aside in a warm place for about 45 minutes to rise to the top of the pan.

6 To make the topping, lightly beat the egg yolk with the milk and superfine sugar and brush over the loaf. Score the top of the bread with 3–4 shallow, diagonal cuts. Arrange the orange peel on the loaf. Bake in a preheated oven, 425°F/220°C, for 35–40 minutes, until golden. Transfer to a wire rack to cool.

WALNUT LOAF

INGREDIENTS

1 cup hand-hot water
5 tsp sunflower oil
1½ tsp walnut oil
1½ tsp chopped basil in oil, drained
2½ cups white bread flour
2½ tbsp nonfat dry milk powder
1½ tsp dried marjoram
1½ tsp dried thyme
1½ tsp salt
2¼ tbsp sugar
1¼ tsp easy-blend dried yeast
2½ oz/70 g walnuts, chopped, and
    whole walnuts for garnish

1 Remove the bread pan from the bread machine. Pour the water into the bread pan and add the sunflower oil, walnut oil, and basil.

2 Sprinkle the flour over the liquid so that it is completely covered then sprinkle in the nonfat dry milk powder and dried herbs. Place the salt and sugar in 2 corners of the pan. Make an indentation in the flour with your finger without exposing the liquid and add the yeast to it.

3 Fit the bread pan in the machine and close the lid. Set the bread machine to the basic setting, medium crust. When the machine beeps, or 5 minutes before the end of kneading, add the chopped walnuts.

4 When the cycle has finished, switch off the machine. Remove the bread pan with oven gloves and turn out the bread on to a wire rack to cool. Top with walnuts if desired. Remove the kneading blade if necessary.

MALTED FRUIT LOAF

INGREDIENTS
scant 1 cup hand-hot water
2 tsp sunflower oil
2 tbsp malt extract (or malt syrup)
$1\frac{1}{2}$ tbsp molasses
$2\frac{1}{2}$ cups plain flour
1 tsp salt
1 tsp easy-blend dried yeast
5 oz/140 g golden raisins

1 Remove the bread pan from the bread machine. Pour the water into the bread pan and add the sunflower oil, malt extract, and molasses.

2 Sprinkle the flour over the liquid so that it is completely covered. Place the salt in 1 corner of the pan. Make an indentation in the flour with your finger without exposing the liquid and add the yeast to it.

3 Fit the bread pan in the machine and close the lid. Set the bread machine to basic setting, medium crust, and switch on. When the machine beeps for extra ingredients, or 5 minutes before the end of kneading, add the golden raisins.

4 When the cycle has finished, switch off the machine. Remove the bread pan with oven gloves and turn out the bread on to a wire rack to cool. Remove the kneading blade if necessary.

ALMOND PASTRIES

INGREDIENTS

Danish pastry
5 tbsp hand-hot milk
2 eggs, one separated
1$\frac{1}{2}$ cups white bread flour, plus
   extra for dusting
$\frac{1}{2}$ tsp salt
1 tbsp superfine sugar
10 tbsp butter, softened
sunflower oil, for greasing
1 tbsp water
slivered almonds, for sprinkling

Filling
1 tbsp butter
$\frac{3}{8}$ cup superfine sugar
1 cup ground almonds
2–3 drops almond extract
1 small egg, beaten lightly

1 First, make the pastry. Remove the bread pan from the bread machine. Pour the milk into the bread pan and add the whole egg. Sprinkle the flour over the liquid. Place the salt, sugar, and 1 oz/25 g of the butter in 3 corners of the pan. Make an indentation in the flour with your finger without exposing the liquid and add the yeast to it. Fit the pan in the machine, close the lid, set it at dough setting and press start. Shape the butter into a $\frac{3}{4}$–inch/2–cm–thick rectangle.

2 Roll out the finished dough into a rectangle twice as long and a little wider than the butter. Place the butter on one half of the dough rectangle, fold the other half over and seal the edges. Roll out again into a rectangle about $\frac{3}{4}$ inch/ 2 cm thick, then fold the top-third down and the bottom-third up and seal the edges. Wrap in plastic wrap and chill for 15 minutes. Repeat the process two more times, wrapping and chilling for 20 minutes each time.

3 To make the filling, cream the butter with the sugar until pale and fluffy. Add the ground almonds and almond essence, then stir in the beaten egg.

4 Lightly beat the white from the separated egg. Roll out the dough into a 16 x 12–inch/40 x 30–cm rectangle and cut into 4–inch/10–cm squares. Spread a little filling on half of each square, brush the edges with the egg white, fold the pastry over the filling and seal. Cut decoratively along the sealed edges and place on an oiled cookie sheet. Cover with oiled plastic wrap and set aside for 30 minutes to rise.

5 Beat the remaining egg yolk with the water and brush over the pastries. Sprinkle with the slivered almonds and bake in a preheated oven, 400˚F/200˚C, for 15 minutes, until golden. Transfer to a wire rack to cool.

PIZZA AND MEDITERRANEAN BREADS

With a bread machine, making perfect pizza dough is simplicity itself. This chapter includes recipes for different kinds of dough. It's up to you whether you make thin-crust or thick-crust, large, or individual pizzas. There is also a recipe for Roasted Vegetable Calzone, a kind of inside-out pizza. The recipes here include a selection of toppings, but you can substitute your favorite ingredients to make pizzas to suit all the family. This chapter also provides recipes for Focaccia with Mozzarella and Rosemary and the classic Provençal recipe made with olives, Pissaladière.

PEPPERONI AND ONION PIZZA

INGREDIENTS

Dough

scant 1 cup hand-hot water

1 tbsp butter, melted

2³⁄₈ cups white bread flour, plus
    extra for dusting

1 tsp salt

2 tbsp sugar

1 tsp easy-blend dried yeast

olive oil, for greasing

Topping

4 tbsp sun-dried tomato paste

4 tomatoes, skinned and sliced thinly

2 red onions, chopped finely

4 slices prosciutto or other cooked
    ham, shredded coarsely

12 slices pepperoni sausage

12 black olives

³⁄₄ tsp dried oregano or herbes
    de Provence

2 oz/55 g mozzarella cheese, grated

olive oil, for drizzling

salt

1 To make the dough, remove the bread pan from the bread machine. Pour the water into the bread pan and add the melted butter. Sprinkle the flour over the liquid so that it is completely covered. Place the salt and sugar in 2 corners of the pan. Make an indentation in the flour with your finger without exposing the liquid and add the yeast to it.

2 Fit the bread pan in the machine and close the lid. Set the bread machine to the pizza dough or dough setting. Press start.

3 When the cycle has finished, switch off the machine. Remove the bread pan. Lightly grease 2 pizza pans or cookie sheets. Lightly flour a work surface and remove the dough from the pan. Knock back gently and divide in half. Roll out each piece of dough into a 10–inch/25–cm round and place on the pizza pans or cookie sheets. Push up the edges slightly to make a thin rim. Cover with lightly oiled plastic wrap and set aside to rest for 15 minutes.

4 To make the topping, spread the sun-dried tomato paste evenly over each pizza base. Arrange the tomato slices on each base and season with salt. Sprinkle over the chopped onion and prosciutto and arrange the pepperoni on top. Add the olives and sprinkle with oregano. Divide the grated cheese between the pizzas and drizzle with olive oil.

5 Bake in a preheated oven, 425°F/220°C, for 20–30 minutes, until golden and sizzling. Serve immediately.

CIABATTA WITH TOMATO AND BASIL

INGREDIENTS

Italian sponge
⁷/₈ cup hand-hot water
1¹/₈ cups white bread flour
¹/₂ tsp easy-blend dried yeast

Dough
⁷/₈ cup hand-hot water
2 tbsp olive oil, plus extra for greasing
2 tbsp milk

2³/₈ cups white bread flour, plus
   extra for dusting
1¹/₂ tsp salt
¹/₂ tsp sugar
¹/₄ tsp easy-blend dried yeast
1¹/₂ oz/40 g drained sun-dried
   tomatoes in oil, chopped roughly
   plus extra for topping if required
2 tbsp shredded fresh basil

1 Remove the bread pan from the bread machine. To make the Italian sponge, pour the water into the bread pan. Sprinkle the flour over the liquid so that it is completely covered. Make an indentation in the flour with your finger without exposing the liquid and add the yeast to it.

2 Fit the bread pan in the machine and close the lid. Set the bread machine to the dough setting and press start. After 5 minutes, switch off the machine and leave the Italian sponge in the pan for 12 hours or overnight.

3 Remove the bread pan. To make the dough, pour the water onto the sponge mixture in the bread pan. Add the olive oil and milk. Sprinkle the flour over the liquid. Place the salt and sugar in 2 corners of the pan. Make an indentation in the flour with your finger without exposing the liquid. Add the yeast.

4 Fit the bread pan in the machine and close the lid. Set the machine to the dough setting and press start. When the machine beeps, or 5 minutes before the end of kneading, add the sun-dried tomatoes and basil. When the cycle has finished, switch off the machine

and remove the bread pan. Transfer the dough to a large bowl, cover with oiled plastic wrap and set aside in a warm place for 1 hour to rise.

5 Halve the dough, using a spoon, and gently tip each half on to 2 lightly floured cookie sheets. Shape each piece of dough into a rectangular loaf about 1 inch/2.5 cm thick. Dust with flour and set aside, uncovered, in a warm place for 30 minutes to rise.

6 Add topping if required. Bake in a preheated oven, 425°F/ 220°C, for 25–30 minutes, until the loaves are golden.

RICOTTA, SPINACH AND PINE NUT PIZZA

INGREDIENTS

Dough

1¼ cups hand-hot water

2 tbsp olive oil, plus extra for greasing

1½ cups white bread flour, plus extra for dusting

1½ cups whole wheat bread flour

1½ tsp salt

½ tsp sugar

1 tsp easy-blend dried yeast

Topping

12 oz/350 g spinach

2 tbsp olive oil, plus extra for drizzling

1 onion, sliced thinly

6 tbsp ricotta cheese

½ tsp freshly grated nutmeg

2 tbsp pine nuts

4 oz/115 g Fontina cheese, sliced thinly

salt and pepper

1 To make the dough, remove the bread pan from the bread machine. Pour the water into the bread pan and add the olive oil. Sprinkle both types of flour over the liquid. Place the salt and sugar in 2 corners of the pan. Make an indentation in the flour with your finger without exposing the liquid and add the yeast to it.

2 Fit the bread pan in the machine and close the lid. Set the bread machine to the pizza dough or dough setting and press start. When the cycle has finished, switch off the machine and remove the bread pan. Lightly flour a work surface and remove the dough from the pan. Knock back gently and divide in half. Roll out each piece of dough into a 12–inch/30–cm–diameter round and place on oiled pizza pans or cookie sheets. Push up the edges to make a thin rim. Cover with oiled plastic wrap and set aside to rest for 15 minutes.

3 To make the topping, wash the spinach in cold water and dry well. Heat the oil in a pan, add the onion and cook until soft and translucent. Add the spinach and cook, stirring, until just wilted. Remove the pan from the heat and drain off any liquid.

4 Spread the ricotta cheese evenly over the pizza bases, then cover with spinach and onion mixture. Sprinkle over the nutmeg and pine nuts and season to taste with salt and pepper. Top with the slices of Fontina and drizzle with olive oil. Bake in a preheated oven, 425˚F/220˚C, for 20–30 minutes, until golden and sizzling. Serve immediately.

OLIVE AND FETA BREAD

INGREDIENTS
generous $^7/_8$ cup hand-hot water
2$^1/_2$ cups white bread flour, plus extra
   for dusting
1 tbsp nonfat dry milk powder
1 tsp salt
1$^1/_2$ tsp sugar
1 tsp easy-blend dried yeast
2 oz/55 g pitted black olives,
   chopped
2 oz/55 g feta cheese, crumbled
olive oil, for brushing and greasing
mixed herbs for garnish

1 Remove the bread pan from the bread machine. Pour the water into the bread pan. Sprinkle the flour over the liquid so that it is completely covered, then sprinkle in the nonfat dry milk powder. Place the salt and sugar in 2 corners of the pan. Make an indentation in the flour with your finger without exposing the liquid and add the yeast to it.

2 Fit the bread pan in the machine and close the lid. Set the bread machine to the dough setting and press start. When the machine beeps, or 5 minutes before the end of kneading, add the olives and feta.

3 When the cycle has finished, switch off the machine and remove the bread pan. Lightly oil a 8–inch/20–cm–diameter round cake pan. Lightly flour a work surface and remove the dough from the pan. Knock back gently, then shape into a round, 8 inches/20 cm in diameter. Ease the dough into the cake pan, cover with lightly oiled plastic wrap and set aside in a warm place for 40–45 minutes to rise.

4 Remove the plastic wrap and brush the top of the loaf with olive oil. Sprinkle with herbs. Bake in a preheated oven, 400°F/200°C, for 35–40 minutes, until the loaf is golden and sounds hollow when tapped on the base. Transfer to a wire rack to cool.

FOCACCIA WITH MOZZARELLA AND ROSEMARY

INGREDIENTS

generous ⁷⁄₈ cup hand-hot water

1 tbsp olive oil, plus extra for greasing

2¹⁄₂ cups white bread flour, plus extra
   for dusting

¹⁄₂ tsp salt

1 tsp sugar

1 tsp easy-blend dried yeast

5 oz/140 g mozzarella cheese, grated

Topping

2 tbsp olive oil

fresh rosemary sprigs

coarse sea salt

1 To make the dough, remove the bread pan from the bread machine. Pour in the water and add the oil. Sprinkle the flour over the liquid. Place the salt and sugar in 2 corners of the pan. Make an indentation in the flour without exposing the liquid. Add the yeast.

2 Fit the bread pan in the machine and close the lid. Set the bread machine to the dough or pizza dough setting and press start.

3 When the cycle has finished, switch off the machine and remove the bread pan. Lightly oil a round, shallow 10–in/25–cm–diameter cake pan and flour the work surface. Remove the dough from the pan, knock back and flatten. Sprinkle over the mozzarella and knead gently to mix. Shape into a ball, flatten slightly, then roll out into a 10–in/25–cm round. Place in the pan, cover with lightly oiled plastic wrap and set

aside in a warm place for 20 minutes to rise.

4 Remove the plastic wrap. Make deep indentations all over the surface of the dough with your fingers. Cover with lightly oiled plastic wrap and set aside in a warm place for 15 minutes to rise.

5 Remove the plastic wrap. For the topping, drizzle the olive oil all over the surface of the dough. Sprinkle with the rosemary sprigs and sea salt. Bake in a preheated oven, 400˚F/200˚C, for 20–25 minutes, until golden. Transfer to a wire rack to cool slightly. Serve warm.

ROASTED VEGETABLE CALZONE

INGREDIENTS

Dough
scant ²/₃ cup hand-hot water
2 tbsp olive oil, plus extra for greasing
    and brushing
1¹/₂ cups white bread flour
1 tsp salt
¹/₂ tsp sugar
1 tsp easy-blend dried yeast

Filling
1 red onion, cut into wedges
2 garlic cloves, skin left on
2 baby eggplants, quartered lengthways
2 zucchini, halved lengthways
1 small red bell pepper, seeded and
    quartered lengthways
1 small orange bell pepper, seeded and
    quartered lengthways
4 tbsp olive oil
1 tbsp balsamic vinegar
1 tbsp chopped fresh parsley
3 oz/85 g goat's cheese, diced
salt and pepper

1 To make the dough, remove the bread pan from the bread machine. Pour the water into the bread pan and add the oil. Sprinkle the flour over the liquid so that it is completely covered. Place the salt and sugar in 2 corners of the pan. Make an indentation in the flour with your finger without exposing the liquid and add the yeast to it.

2 Fit the bread pan in the machine and close the lid. Set the machine to the pizza dough or dough setting and press start.

3 When the cycle has finished, switch off the machine. Remove the bread pan. Lightly oil a large cookie sheet. Lightly flour a work surface and remove the dough from the pan. Knock back gently and divide in half. Roll out each piece of dough into a round about ¹/₄ inch/ 5 mm thick and place on the cookie sheet. Cover with lightly oiled plastic wrap and set aside to rest for 15 minutes.

4 Meanwhile, make the filling. Place the onion, garlic, eggplants, zucchini, and red and orange bell peppers in a roasting pan. Combine the olive oil, balsamic vinegar, and parsley in a bowl and season to taste with salt and pepper. Pour the oil mixture over the vegetables and toss to coat. Roast in a preheated oven, 400°F/200°C, turning once, for about 15 minutes. Remove from the oven and set aside to cool.

5 Peel off the skins from the garlic and peppers. Divide the vegetable mixture in half. Place 1 portion of vegetables on half of each dough round, leaving a ¹/₂–inch/1–cm border. Sprinkle half of the goat's cheese over each portion of filling. Brush the edges of the dough with water, fold the uncovered halves over and seal the edges. Brush with oil and bake in a preheated oven, 425°F/220°C, for 20–30 minutes, until golden. Serve immediately.

PISSALADIÈRE

INGREDIENTS
scant ¹/₂ cup hand-hot water
1 egg, beaten lightly
1¹/₂ cups white bread flour, plus
extra for dusting
1 tsp salt
2 tbsp butter, softened or diced
1 tsp easy-blend dried yeast
olive oil, for greasing

Topping
3 tsp olive oil
1 lb 2 oz/500 g red onions,
sliced thinly
2 garlic cloves, chopped finely
2 tsp superfine sugar
1¹/₂ tbsp balsamic vinegar
3¹/₂ oz/100 g canned anchovy
fillets, drained
12 black olives
1 tsp dried marjoram
salt and pepper

1 To make the dough, remove the bread pan from the bread machine. Pour the water into the bread pan and add the egg. Sprinkle the flour over the liquid so that it is completely covered. Place the salt and butter in 2 corners of the pan. Make an indentation in the flour with your finger without exposing the liquid and add the yeast to it.

2 Fit the bread pan in the machine and close the lid. Set the bread machine to the pizza dough or dough setting and press start.

3 Meanwhile, make the topping. Heat the oil in a large, heavy-based skillet. Add the onions and garlic and cook over a low heat, stirring occasionally, for about 30 minutes, until golden. Add the sugar and vinegar and season to taste with salt and pepper. Cook, stirring frequently, for about 5 minutes, then remove the pan from the heat and set aside to cool.

4 When the cycle has finished, switch off the machine and remove the bread pan. Lightly oil a 11 x 8–inch/28 x 20–cm Swiss roll pan. Lightly flour the work surface and remove the dough from the pan. Knock back gently, then roll out into a 12 x 9–inch/30 x 23–cm rectangle. Lift the dough into the pan and ease into place so that it lines the base and sides.

5 Spread the onion mixture evenly over the base of the dough. Arrange the anchovy fillets in a criss-cross pattern on top and place the olives in between them. Sprinkle with the marjoram. Cover with lightly oiled plastic wrap and set aside in a warm place for 10–15 minutes to rise.

6 Remove the plastic wrap and bake in a preheated oven, 400˚F/200˚C, for 25–30 minutes, until the dough is golden. Serve hot or warm.

MUFFINS

INGREDIENTS

1½ cups hand-hot milk
3½ cups white bread flour,
   or 1½ cups white bread
   flour plus 1½ cups whole wheat
   bread flour, plus extra
   for dusting

1½ tsp salt
1 tsp superfine sugar
1 tbsp butter, softened or diced
1½ tsp easy-blend dried yeast
ground rice or rice flour, for dusting
sunflower oil, for greasing

1 Remove the bread pan from the bread machine. Pour the milk into the pan. Sprinkle the flour over the liquid so that it is completely covered. Place the salt, sugar, and butter in 3 corners of the pan. Make an indentation in the flour with your finger without exposing the liquid and add the yeast to it.

2 Fit the bread pan in the machine and close the lid. Set the bread machine to the dough setting and press start.

3 When the cycle has finished, switch off the machine and remove the bread pan. Lightly flour a work surface and remove the dough from the pan. Knock back gently, then roll out to ½ inch/1 cm thick. Stamp out rounds with a 3-inch/ 7.5–cm plain pastry cutter. Gather up the trimmings, knead together and leave to rest for 3–4 minutes. Re-roll and stamp out another 1 or 2 muffins.

4 Dust a cookie sheet with ground rice and place the muffins on it. Dust the tops with ground rice. Cover with oiled plastic wrap and set aside in a warm place for 20–25 minutes to rise.

5 Remove the plastic wrap. Oil a griddle pan or heavy skillet and heat well. Cook the muffins in batches, over a low heat, for 6–7 minutes on each side. Serve warm.

HONEY AND PECAN TEA BREAD

INGREDIENTS

½ cup hand-hot milk

¾ cup mandarin or orange yogurt,
    at room temperature

3 tbsp clear honey

3¾ cups white bread flour

¾ tsp salt

3 tbsp butter, softened or diced

1½ tsp easy-blend yeast

1½ oz/40 g pecan nuts, chopped

1 tbsp grated orange rind, optional

1 Remove the bread pan from the bread machine. Pour the milk into the bread pan and add the yogurt and honey.

2 Sprinkle the flour over the liquid so that it is completely covered. Place the salt and butter in 2 corners of the pan. Make an indentation in the flour with your finger without exposing the liquid and add the yeast to it.

3 Fit the bread pan in the machine and close the lid. Set the bread machine to the basic setting, medium crust, and press start. When the machine beeps for extra ingredients, or 5 minutes before the end of kneading, add the pecan nuts and orange rind, if using.

4 When the cycle has finished, switch off the machine. Remove the bread pan with oven gloves and turn out the bread on to a wire rack to cool. Remove the kneading blade if necessary.

CREAMY SPLITS

INGREDIENTS

²/₃ cup hand-hot milk

1¹/₂ cups white bread flour, plus
    extra for dusting

¹/₂ tsp salt

2 tbsp superfine sugar

1 tsp easy-blend dried yeast

sunflower oil, for greasing

confectioners' sugar, for dusting

Filling
strawberry jelly
double cream, whipped stiffly

1 Remove the bread pan from the bread machine. Pour the milk into the pan. Sprinkle the flour over the liquid so that it is completely covered. Place the salt and sugar in 2 corners of the pan. Make an indentation in the flour with your finger without exposing the liquid and add the yeast to it.

2 Fit the bread pan in the machine and close the lid. Set the bread machine to the dough setting and press start.

3 When the cycle has finished, switch off the machine and remove the bread pan. Lightly oil 2 cookie sheets. Lightly flour a work surface, remove the dough from the pan and knock back gently.

4 Divide the dough into 8 equal pieces and shape each one into a ball with your hands. Place on the cookie sheets and flatten the tops slightly. Cover with lightly oiled plastic wrap and set aside in a warm place for about 45 minutes to rise.

5 Remove the plastic wrap and bake the buns in a preheated oven, 425°F/220°C, for about 15 minutes, until golden. Transfer to a wire rack to cool completely.

6 When the splits are cold, cut them open and fill with strawberry jelly and cream. Dust with confectioners' sugar and serve.

COFFEE CAKE WITH BRANDY

INGREDIENTS

5 tbsp strong black coffee
2 tbsp brandy
1 cinnamon stick
4 oz/115 g raisins
2 tbsp hand-hot milk
3 eggs
3³/₄ cups white bread flour

¹/₂ tsp salt
³/₈ cup superfine sugar
2 tsp easy-blend dried yeast
6 tbsp butter, melted,
    plus extra for greasing
sunflower oil, for greasing
2 egg whites
confectioners' sugar, for dusting

1 Pour the coffee into a small saucepan, add the brandy and the cinnamon stick. Heat to just below boiling point, then remove from the heat. Add the raisins and set aside for 30 minutes, until the raisins have plumped up and the liquid has cooled to hand-hot.

2 Remove the bread pan from the bread machine. Pour the milk into the bread pan and strain in the coffee mixture. Discard the cinnamon stick and reserve the raisins. Add the whole eggs to the pan. Sprinkle the flour over the liquid so that it is completely covered. Place the salt and sugar in 2 corners of the pan. Make an indentation in the flour with your finger without exposing the liquid and add the yeast to it.

3 Fit the bread pan in the machine and close the lid. Set the bread machine to the dough setting and press start. After 5 minutes, add one-third of the melted butter, then close the lid. After 10 minutes, add half of the melted butter. After 15 minutes, add all the remaining butter.

4 When the cycle has finished, switch off the machine. Remove the bread pan and turn out the dough into a large mixing bowl. Gently knead in the reserved raisins.

Grease a large brioche mold with butter. Whisk the egg whites in a grease-free bowl into soft peaks. Gradually incorporate the egg whites into the dough, folding in gently. Spoon the dough into the brioche mold, cover with oiled plastic wrap and set aside in a warm place for 1¹/₄–1¹/₂ hours to rise.

5 Remove the plastic wrap and bake in a preheated oven, 375°F/190°C, for 55–60 minutes, until the surface is firm to the touch and a skewer inserted into the cake comes out clean. Turn the cake out on to a wire rack to cool, then dust with confectioners' sugar before serving.

SAFFRON HONEY BREAD

INGREDIENTS
1 tsp saffron threads
$^7/_8$ cup milk
2 eggs, beaten lightly
3$^3/_4$ cups white bread flour, plus
   extra for dusting
$^1/_2$ tsp salt

4 tbsp superfine sugar
4 tbsp butter, melted
1 tsp easy-blend dried yeast
sunflower oil, for greasing

Glaze
1–2 tbsp clear honey

1 Place the saffron threads in a small bowl. Heat 5 tablespoons of the milk in a small saucepan, pour it over the saffron and set aside for at least 30 minutes.

2 Remove the bread pan from the bread machine. Pour the saffron milk and remaining unflavored milk into the pan and add the eggs. Sprinkle the flour over the liquid so that it is completely covered. Place the salt, sugar and butter in 3 corners of the pan. Make an indentation in the flour with your finger without exposing the liquid and add the yeast to it.

3 Fit the bread pan in the machine and close the lid. Set the bread machine to the dough setting and press start.

4 When the cycle has finished, switch off the machine and remove the bread pan. Lightly oil a cookie sheet. Lightly flour a work surface and remove the dough from the pan. Knock back gently, then divide into 2 pieces. Roll each piece of dough into a rope about 18 inches/46 cm long. Place the ropes side by side and, starting at the center, twist 1 rope of dough around the other. Continue twisting until you reach the ends. Turn the dough around and twist the ropes at

the other end. Dampen the ends with water and tuck them under the loaf to seal.

5 Place the loaf on the cookie sheet, cover with oiled plastic wrap and set aside in a warm place for about 1 hour to rise.

6 Heat the honey for the glaze until it is runny. Remove the plastic wrap and brush the top of the loaf with the honey. Bake in a preheated oven, 375°F/190°C for 20 minutes. Lower the oven temperature to 350°F/180°C and bake for a further 10–15 minutes, until golden. Transfer to a wire rack to cool.

CINNAMON AND SPICE BREAD

INGREDIENTS

2$\frac{1}{2}$ cups plain flour

1$\frac{1}{2}$ tsp baking powder

$\frac{1}{4}$ tsp salt

1 tsp ground cinnamon

$\frac{1}{2}$ tsp mixed spice

$\frac{1}{2}$ tsp freshly grated nutmeg

$\frac{1}{2}$ tsp ground ginger

4 tbsp butter

4 tbsp molasses

3 eggs, beaten lightly

$\frac{1}{4}$ cup milk

1 oz/25 g raisins

2 oz/55 g dried apple rings,
    snipped into pieces

1 Sift the flour, baking powder, salt, and spices into a mixing bowl and set aside.

2 Put the butter and molasses into a saucepan over a low heat, stirring constantly, until the butter has melted. Leave to cool slightly, then stir in the eggs, milk, raisins, and apple pieces. Add the molasses mixture to the flour mixture and stir gently until combined.

3 Remove the bread pan from the bread machine. Turn the mixture into the bread pan, fit the pan in the machine and close the lid. Set the bread machine to the cake setting and press start.

4 When the cycle has finished, switch off the machine. Remove the bread pan with oven gloves and turn out the bread on to a wire rack to cool. Remove the kneading blade if necessary.

PAINS AUX CHOCOLAT

INGREDIENTS

½ cup hand-hot water
1¾ cups white bread flour
2 tbsp nonfat dry milk powder
½ tsp salt
1 tbsp superfine sugar
10 tbsp butter, softened, plus
   extra for greasing

1½ tsp easy-blend dried yeast
sunflower oil, for greasing
8 oz/225 g semisweet chocolate,
   broken into pieces

Glaze
1 egg yolk
1 tsp milk

1 Remove the pan from the bread machine. Pour in the water. Sprinkle the flour over the liquid, then sprinkle in the milk powder. Place the salt, sugar and 1 oz/25 g of the butter in 3 corners of the pan. Make an indentation in the flour with your finger and add the yeast to it. Fit the pan in the machine, close the lid, set at dough setting and press start. Shape the remaining butter into a rectangle about ¾ inch/2 cm thick.

2 Knock the finished dough back gently. Shape into a ball and cut a cross in the center halfway down through the dough. Roll out the edges of the dough, leaving the cross untouched. Place the butter rectangle in the center and fold the rolled-out edges over it, pressing to seal. Roll out the dough again into a long rectangle. Fold the top-third of dough down and the bottom-third up and seal the edges. Wrap the dough in oiled plastic wrap and chill in the refrigerator for 20 minutes. Repeat twice more, rolling from the left-hand edge each time, and finally chill for 30 minutes.

3 Roll out the dough into a 21 x 12–inch/53 x 30–cm rectangle. Cut lengthways into 3 strips, then widthways to make 9 equal rectangles. Place a few chocolate pieces on the short end of each rectangle. Beat the egg yolk with the milk and brush the glaze around the edges of the dough. Roll up the dough to enclose the chocolate and seal the edges. Transfer to oiled cookie sheets, seam-side down. Cover with oiled plastic wrap and set aside in a warm place for 30 minutes to rise.

4 Remove the plastic wrap and brush the tops of the pastries with the remaining glaze. Bake in a preheated oven, 400°F/200°C, for 15 minutes, until golden. Transfer to a wire rack. Serve warm.